A Nail in a Sure Place

Dr. C. W. Powell

"The words of the wise are as goads, and as nails
fastened by the masters of assemblies,
which are given by one shepherd."
--Ecclesiastes 12:11

Fig Publishing
6050 Del Paz Drive
Colorado Springs, CO 80918
All Rights Reserved
Second Printing, 1994
Third Printing, 1996
Second Edition: 2015

Cover by Melody De Filippo

All Bible quotations are from the KJV The border around the cover picture is taken from the original cover on the First Edition, which showed a "School Crossing" sign with the caption, "Beware, Children Crossing."

As a Wife and Mother

As a teacher and mother of little ones, I found *A Nail in a Sure Place* to be a very encouraging book. There are many wise proverbs that speak to teachers and young parents, but the tone in which Dr. Powell writes about them really hit home for me. "...we need to recognize that God has a time schedule for each child. Each will bear fruit in God's own time...they will grow in God's time and according to His purpose." "We cannot know what the will of God is for each student, but we can learn in part to discern aptitude and gifts." "The sin of pride is to usurp the place of God." Our children and those we teach are not our own, but God has placed them in our care for a time, for His glory.

Expecting all children to behave and perform the same despite their many differences is a major flaw in modern education. I have read many classroom management and parenting books that claim if you only follow their plan, your students or children will automatically fall into line. Dr. Powell makes no such claim, but he does point to Biblical truths that may help you along the way. I have kept this book on my bedside table, and I continue to reread it seeking the comfort and encouragement provided in Bible proverbs. Seeking out the Scriptures quoted has helped me tremendously.

Melody DeFilippo. Teacher and Mother.

Contents

Dedication

To Penny, my wife of more than 50 years, loyal companion, faithful critic, and dedicated colleague, a master educator in her own right.

"Her Price is far above rubies. The heart of her husband doth safely trust in her." Proverbs 31:10,11

To the Northstate Pioneers, Those 19 hardy students who were the first graduates of Northstate High School, in Anderson, California., and to the memories that were made, 1961-1986

Other Comments by Educators

"I was blessed to have C.W. Powell as a teacher, a mentor, an administrator, and a role model for my entire K-12 education years. I was provided with the opportunity to learn the proper curriculum - as well as Godly principles to guide me throughout my life. As a public school educator today, I recall daily examples from Pastor Powell that I am able to incorporate into my time with my students."

--**Brian Brickey**, Redding, California. Northstate Pioneer

∞

What a blessing to read Dr. Powell's book, "A Nail in a Sure Place" a second time! I read it once before nearly twenty years ago. The wisdom from the book of Proverbs, explained through the wisdom of Dr. Powell will hone the teaching skills of any educator or parent! Thank you for sharing these precious thoughts with us, Dr. Powell.

--**Mr. Dale Hart**, Second Grade Teacher and Assistant Principal, The Evangelical Christian Academy (ECA), Colorado Springs, CO).

A Nail in a Sure Place
Introduction

"The words of the wise are as goads, and as nails
fastened by the masters of assemblies, which are given
from one shepherd."
--Ecclesiastes 12:11

What a wonderful scripture for a school teacher!

The word "fastened" is a figurative use of the word for "plant." A tree is planted, the roots go down deep, and the storms cannot uproot it. The nail is "planted" in the wood and secures the house for centuries. Wise words fastened in the heart will secure the heart for eternity.

This is especially important in early childhood. Studies have shown that a good first-grade teacher sets the pattern for years in the life of a child. "I can read," "I can do math," "I love history" are joyful cries of confidence that will bring immense rewards for a lifetime. The wise teacher will nail this confidence down. What is faith but confidence: confidence rooted in a sense of God's mercy and favor?

Oxen are faithful, stolid, obedient workers, but must often be "goaded" in order to get maximum production. A child may also need to be "pushed" or "encouraged" to go in the right direction. Wise words can do this. This is not the same as carping and nagging. An insecure child will often not respond well to "goads" that do nothing but reinforce feelings of failure. True wisdom will fit the "goad" to the individual student.

When teachers become "masters of assemblies," and are skillful in the use of the words given by the "One Shepherd" Jesus Christ, then our schools will become islands of sanity and security. They will provide the peace that makes possible the fruit of righteousness (James 3:18).

This is the reason for this book. It is not the purpose of this book to give the teacher more ideas for what to do TO the class. There are many such books. This book, hopefully, will help make teachers better and wiser people. They will do less TO their classes, perhaps, and accomplish much more.

The author has more than fifty years of experience as a teacher, administrator, promoter of Christian schools and education. A lifetime of study and meditation has convinced him that the Scripture, and especially the book of Proverbs, contains the wisdom that the teacher needs to provide this secure, encouraging training. This book will share with you some of the results of that study.

1994, Colorado Springs.   Revised, 2015
C. W. Powell

Chapter One:
The Very Best Medicine

"A merry heart maketh a cheerful countenance: but by sorrow of the heart the spirit is broken." --Proverbs 15:13

"A merry heart doeth good like a medicine: but a broken spirit drieth the bones." --Proverbs 17:22.

"Keep thy heart with all diligence; for out of it are the issues of life."
--Proverbs 4:23

"As in water face answereth to face, so the heart of man to man."
--Proverbs 27:19

What makes a good teacher? The question is similar to one that a lawyer once asked Jesus, "What is the greatest commandment?" Jesus did not fall into the trap of comparing one commandment with another, but summarized the whole law as consisting of love to God and to our neighbor (Matthew 22:36-40).

In a similar fashion, we might summarize the qualifications of a good teacher as one who has a good heart--a merry heart.

Why is it that some classrooms are happy, cheerful, and productive, and others are resentful, sullen and failing? In practically every case, the reason is the attitude of the classroom teacher. A teacher can see his attitude reflected in the class just as he could see his face in a pool of water. A tense, angry teacher will have a tense, angry class. If the teacher is cheerful, enthusiastic, and confident, the class will be also.

Jesus said, "A good man out of the good treasure of his heart bringeth forth that which is good; and an evil man out of the evil treasure of his heart bringeth forth that which is evil: for of the abundance of the heart his mouth speaketh" (Luke 6:45).

What are the characteristics of a good heart? First of all, a good heart is a **new** heart. When a man is right with God, the stony heart of unbelief and rebellion is taken away and replaced with a heart of obedience (Jeremiah 31:33; Ezekiel 36:26; Hebrews 10:16).

This new heart is a **joyful** heart. The joy of the Lord is the strength of the believer (Nehemiah 8:10). It is a great sin to serve the Lord in grumpiness and bitterness. Israel was carried away captive by their enemies because they did not serve the Lord with "joyfulness and with gladness of heart" (Deuteronomy 28:47-48). The peace that comes with trust in Christ and confidence in the grace of God is the soil from which all the beautiful fruit of righteousness grows (James 3:17,18). The teacher who has wars and fighting within her heart will have wars and fighting within her classroom (James 4:1,2).

A good heart is a **true** heart. There must be no question about loyalty to Jesus Christ and his word, to our students, to parents, to fellow teachers, to the institution where we work. Jesus said that we cannot serve two masters. In this context he said, if "thine eye be single, thy whole body shall be full of light. But if thine eye be evil, thy whole body shall be full of darkness" (Matthew 6:22-23). A double eye is an evil eye.

There is nothing that will build morale better in a class than for the student (and his parents) to know that the teacher supports, loves, and encourages him, and does not downgrade or belittle him even in her own mind. There is never any contradiction between loyalty to God and loyalty to the people He has placed around us, for those who love God will love His image in their neighbor (1 John 4:20-21).

A true heart is also an **honest** heart. The joy of the Lord cannot be faked, and students have a radar that picks up hypocrisy from a great distance.

Even the best teacher will feel down at times, and things will sometimes upset. Even so, there is a great difference between a joyful person who has troubles at times and a grumpy person who sees everything and every person through bitter eyes.

A good heart speaks good and helpful things. "The mouth of a righteous man is a well of life: but violence covereth the mouth of the wicked" (Proverbs 10:11). Some of the most painful memories your author has from a child were hurtful, violent words that were spoken to him by teachers and others. Only after many years have these memories begun to fade. I also have some wonderful memories of words that still refresh as a cool drink from a deep well.

Our hearts are made good by the implanting of God's word. By hiding God's word in our hearts we keep ourselves from sin (Psalm 119:11). When we "keep" our hearts (Proverbs 4:23), we are guarding and fortifying them with scripture that we might be kept from sin.

A good heart is a **humble** heart. Those who teach others are to "show out of a good conversation his works with meekness of wisdom. But if ye have bitter envying and strife in your hearts, glory not, and lie not against the truth" (James 3:13-14).

Good teaching is win-win. Good students make a teacher look good; and good teaching makes students look good. Teachers are not lords, but helpers to the faith of young Christians.

Many years ago during a time of great testing, I wrote these few sentences and pinned them on the bulletin board in my office, where they remain until this day:

"The greatest victories are not those which we win over circumstances or over others. The really big victories are those which we win over ourselves. The quiet joy of the victories won over weariness, discouragement, and bitterness will last a life time, long after the tinsel crowns and the gilded trophies are forgotten by all,"

Chapter Two:
How Do You Measure?

"A just weight and balance are the Lord's: all the weights of the bag are his work." --Proverbs 16:11

"Divers weights, and divers measures, both of them are alike abomination to the Lord." --Proverbs 20:10

"Mrs. Brown, Martha took my crayons." "Miss Jones, Billy keeps poking me with his pencil." Only a parent, perhaps, has more occasions to be prosecutor, jury, and judge with duty to mete out rewards and punishment than does a school teacher. Few parents, though, have from 20 to 30 children.

In the Proverbs cited above, the immediate subject is fairness in trade, but the underlying subject is that a just God requires us to work for justice wherever we are, including the classroom. Children have a finely-tuned sense of justice and become resentful and bitter if treated unfairly.

Children do not mind strong punishments, if they believe them to be fair, but will become upset over even minor punishments, if they are perceived to be unjust. The teachers who are most bitterly resented are not the "strict" ones (who often are respected), but the unfair ones.

What makes a fair teacher? First of all, the measure must be **clear**. When we pay for a pound of butter, we expect to get a full pound. By act of Congress, the Bureau of Weights and Measures in Washington, D. C., has defined the pound, and both merchants and consumer are expected to know what it is. It is also true that God has clearly established His standards in the Bible, so that we are all without excuse, and in the last day every mouth shall be stopped (Romans 3:19).

Children must know clearly what is expected of them. That is, they must know the standard to which they are accountable. Assignments must be clear, due dates must be definite, standards of behavior must be perfectly clear.

But more than clarity is involved. If we are to be fair, then the standard must be **Biblical**. Ultimately, human authority, including the authority of the teacher, rests upon the authority of God (Romans 13:1). The conscience of the child is God's creation, and is given by God to respond to God's word.

The conscience will be disoriented if it is called to another standard. Our Christian children are the Lord's sheep, and they will not hear the voice of another shepherd (John 10:5). It is, therefore, absolutely essential that the teacher be grounded thoroughly in the doctrines and understanding of the Bible, so that her standards are the standards of Scripture. Tyranny is the imposing of our own agenda and standards on God's people; the only authority we have is in terms of God's agenda and God's standards, as they are revealed in Scripture. God is the only law-giver.

The other side of the coin should give us great confidence, for Biblical authority is real authority, backed up by the Holy Spirit and the conscience. We can teach with real authority and expect to see changes take place in the minds and hearts of children, as we hold before them the clear standards of the Word of God.

The conscience of a man is a great ally for the triumph of righteousness, as it is enlisted on the side of righteousness by the Word and Spirit of God, not by self-appointed regulators of morality.

"The spirit of man is the candle of the Lord, searching all the inward parts of the belly." -- Proverbs 20:27

The third principle of fairness is **proportion**. In law we say that the punishment must fit the crime. The U. S. Bill of Rights forbids imposing "cruel and unusual" punishments. There is a much maligned portion of Biblical law that established the concept of fairness: "Eye for eye, tooth for tooth, hand for hand, foot for foot, burning for burning, wound for wound, stripe for stripe" (Exodus 21:23,24).

The Pharisees misapplied this Scripture to justify getting revenge, and Jesus corrected their thinking by saying that getting even must never be a standard for personal ethics (Matthew 5:38ff). But he also said that we must not "strain at gnats and swallow camels." This means we must have a sense of fairness and justice in what we do and we must be able to tell the difference between a gnat and a camel.

Teachers sometimes get out of control and become severe and harsh over petty offenses. God has given us only so much moral and spiritual capital and it must be used wisely. If you go to war over petty matters, you will use up your moral capital and not have the strength to win the major spiritual battles.

Some offenses deserve a look (my mother was good at that!), some a rebuke, some a lecture, some a detention, some a call to parents, some a suspension, and some an expulsion. We are not to take a life for an eye, nor an eye for a tooth. The punishment must fit the crime. This is the reason the Bible exhorts and commands us to seek wisdom, for it takes much wisdom for a teacher to do this.

Even slave-owners in Israel were forbidden to rule with "rigor" (Lev. 25:43). This rule is repeated in Ephesians 6:9, where masters are urged to "forbear threatening," or "loosen up on your threatening." The rule of Christ is a mild and gentle one, and if we are to be kind and considerate of our servants, how much more our children. We do not have slaves nowadays, but we have hired employees.

Proportion also requires us to see the great differences between children. Some are strong-willed; some are emotionally volatile, some are placid; some have quick intelligence, others move slowly. Jesus said that some of us receive five talents; others receive only one. God's standard is faithfulness, and it must be ours also.

There are many kinds of intelligence. In school we put emphasis on verbal and math skills, and some children simply do not have strength in these fields. God made some with physical dexterity--for some must fight Goliath and his brothers. Some are given sensitivity to the needs of others; some have an eye for beauty in form, color, or music. May God give us wisdom not to try to squeeze some child into a mold that God has not meant him to fill! He will fit perfectly when he finds his place, and our job is to try to help him find it.

The fourth thing to consider is **generosity**, compassion and mercy. Jesus said "Give, and it shall be given unto you; good measure, pressed down, and shaken together, and running over, shall men give into your bosom. For with what measure that ye mete withal it shall be measured to you again" (Luke 6:38). Justice and fairness are established with mercy.

Our dealings with each other are to be generous, not only in business, but also in moral and spiritual things. This means, that I expect to treat others fairly, but do not insist upon strict fairness for myself. Every wrong does not have to be righted, and every sin does not have to be judged. We are only to bear witness of the truth, and to maintain such order that will enable us to live together in peace. The rest we are to leave to God, who will require an accounting from all of us.

The good-hearted teacher, who loves her students, who is generous with their faults and faithful in her witness, and who keeps such order as is required for good instructions will in turn be loved by her students and will leave memories that will last a

Chapter Three:
The Times and Seasons

"He that blesseth his friend with a loud voice, rising early
in the morning, it shall be counted a curse to him."
--Proverbs 27:14

Smart people not only know what to do, they also
know when to do it. I like the praise of my friends
as well as anyone, but my best friend will be met
with a fishing boot if he comes to praise me at 4:00
o'clock in the morning.

Time is a factor in the success or failure of any
enterprise. Some believe that Napoleon lost the
battle of Waterloo because one of his generals was
late in bringing up his troops. The successful
farmer knows that there is a time to plow, a time to
plant, and a time to fertilize.

A used car dealer, a friend of mine, told me once
that certain types of cars sell better at certain times.
He always wanted to have a good supply of
cheaper, older cars in February and March because
in his area the demand was great during those
months. A business man will not be in business
long if he does not factor time into his sales
equations.

Even the successful cook knows when to beat the mixture, when to let it sit, when to heat it, when to let it cool.

There is a famous passage in Ecclesiastes 2:

"To everything there is a season, and a time to every purpose under the heaven: A time to be born, and a time to die; a time to plant, and a time to pluck up that which is planted; a time to kill, and a time to heal; a time to break down, and a time to build up; a time to weep, and a time to laugh; a time to mourn, and a time to dance; a time to cast away stones, and a time to gather stones together; a time to embrace, and a time to refrain from embracing; a time to get, and a time to lose; a time to keep, and a time to cast away; a time to rend, and a time to sew; a time to keep silence, and a time to speak; a time to love, and a time to hate; a time of war, and a time of peace" (Ecclesiastes 2:1-8).

Some people always seem to know what to say at the right time. (They are a rare breed!) Others always seem to be blurting out the wrong thing at the wrong time. Some of the wisest seem to know when to sit in silence, when to speak soothing words, and when to give the sharp rebuke.

One of the things that most amazed me when I began teaching was how fast the time flew by.

There never seemed to be enough time for all the things I wanted to do during the day. I always seemed to be fighting the clock. I also talked a lot: after all, I had so many wonderful things that the children needed to know. Time was my enemy; I was not wise enough to make it my friend.

When I was little, my father always planted a garden. One spring he gave me a few seeds to plant in a small plot next to his garden. I planted them carefully, trying to do it just as he did. Then several times every day for the next week or so, I scratched around the ground to see if the seeds were growing. My garden was unsuccessful. I learned that you must leave the seeds alone, to make time your friend.

In a little understood parable, our Lord spoke of a householder who went early in the morning to hire laborers for his vineyard (Matthew 20). He agreed to pay them a penny for the day. At other times during the day he hired others, finally taking on workers at the last hour of the day. He paid them all a penny, claiming that he had the right to do what he wanted with his own.

In the parable, Jesus is claiming more than the right to give rewards as He chooses. He is also claiming to be Lord of time. Some become Christians early in life, and serve the Lord all their lives. Others are called in youth; some in middle age; still others are called in advanced years.

As Lord, Jesus not only decides what His servants are to do, but when they are to do it. The rewards are therefore his, and he gives to each of His servants the gift of eternal life. Eternal life does not depend upon the length of service, but the fact of service, for the calling is of grace. Jesus ends this parable with a not-so-subtle warning to the Pharisees, "The last shall be first, and the first last: for many be called, but few chosen" (Matthew 20:16).

There are many ways to apply this major Bible doctrine.

First of all, we need to recognize that God has a time schedule for each child. Each will bear fruit in God's own time. That sullen boy who seems to quarrel with everyone may preach the Gospel someday with tears. That quiet, introspective little boy who seems such an oddball may be a writer of Christian literature and inspire many. The boy who took so long to learn to read may become a most skilled auto mechanic. The girl with those dismal math skills may change the direction of art for a hundred years.

The teacher must not be digging them up continually to see how they grow; they will grow in God's time and according to His purpose. The radish can never grow to be a carrot and some flowers only bloom each century. The seeds of the giant sequoias of California germinate only after the forest fire.

In short, the times and season are in the Lord's hand (Acts 1:7). We cannot know what the will of God is for each student, but we can learn in part to discern aptitude and gifts.

In another context the great Apostle Paul said, "I have planted, Apollos watered; but God gave the increase (1 Corinthians 3:6). The teacher must see himself as a planter and a waterer. Someone else will see the increase, perhaps, but the harvest, too, is in God's hands.

Another way to apply the doctrine of Times and Seasons is to be alert for those golden moments of teaching opportunity. In God's providence a window of opportunity will open for teaching certain lessons. The most effective teaching will take place when this window is open.

Has a student made a trip overseas? Is a family building a new house? Is the farm family preparing a beef for the freezer? These and many other events are taking place every day, and some of them will provide windows of opportunity. Has a favorite relative passed away? Has a family been delivered from a fire or auto accident?

The teacher, as any Christian ought, must see such things as coming from the hand of God. The teacher can turn these things to advantage, to teach lessons about this world, and also lessons about the world to come.

Care must be used to avoid forcing such things, however. The key is to discern the event that rivets the student's attention, softens his heart, and opens his mind to reality and truth. At such moments it might be well to cast away the lesson plans and do some real teaching!

The greatest teacher who ever lived was Jesus Christ. It is instructive to examine his teaching method. Only on a few occasions did he ever deliver a formal presentation. Instead, he was very much in tune with the Times and Seasons. Do women bring their babies to be blessed? He teaches that we must become as little children to enter the kingdom of heaven (Matthew 18:1ff). Does a rich man go way very sorrowfully? Christ teaches about the deceitfulness of riches (Luke 18:18ff). Does he find a fig tree that has no fruit, but only leaves? Our Lord teaches about the power of faith (Mark 11:12ff). Such examples could be multiplied. Jesus made the Times and Seasons work for him.

A Christian philosophy of time demands that we recognize that God is the Creator of time. Time exists in God; God does not exist in time. "Remember the former things of old: for I am God, and there is none else: I am God and there is none like me. Declaring the end from the beginning, and from ancient times the things that are not yet done, saying, My counsel shall stand, and I will do all my pleasure" (Isaiah 46:9,10).

To resist the times and seasons is as foolish as to defy the laws of mathematics and physics. Even Jesus did not come into the world until the time was right (Galatians 4:4).

Sometimes even the folk songs of the world touch on eternal principle. This is one reason why some art and literature never goes out of style but endure. One hit by a country singer is such, though couched in a worldly metaphor. Entitled the "Gambler," part of it goes,

> You gotta know when to hold,
> Know when to fold;
> Know when to walk away,

Know when to run….

One of the greatest blessings God can give to us is an ability to discern the Times and Seasons. It was said of the men of Issachar that they had "understanding of the times, to know what Israel ought to do" (1 Chronicles 12:32). The good teacher knows the Times and Seasons.

Chapter Four:
Do You Know the Right Answer?

"He that answereth a matter before he heareth it, it is folly and shame unto him." --Proverbs 18:13

"A man hath joy by the answer of his mouth: and a word spoken in due season, how good it is!" --Proverbs 15:23

"Why did Mary get to go home early?" may seem an innocent enough question, but it might be a trap. The real question might be quite different from that which is asked, and a teacher ought to know what the real question is before he tries to answer.

This writer has been a school teacher for over fifty years, and I almost fell into this hole the very week that I first wrote this. I called a freshman algebra student to the board to do the solution to a homework assignment. When he was almost finished, I asked the class if he was proceeding correctly. The general opinion was that he was wrong, and a cursory examination of his solution seemed to indicate that. I was about to ask him to start over, when I looked a little closer and realized that he was doing it correctly, but from a perspective different from what I had taught.

At the start, the student had set up the problem in a way that closely resembled the most common mistake made by students working that kind of example. I think the student was playing a game with me, and I almost took his bait. When I was a young teacher, I would have swallowed it hook, line, and sinker, but I have since learned

Learn Proverbs 18:13 "He that answereth a matter before he heareth it, it is folly and shame unto him" and try to follow it: Learn what the question is before you answer. Do not render judgment until you have heard the matter. This student actually understood the principles much better than some who used the traditional solution.

In the average classroom there is a wide range of intelligence, imagination, emotional maturity, and social skills. It is very likely that several children, at least, will have greater natural intelligence than the teacher.

There is nothing that sets apart a great teacher from an ordinary or poor teacher than the quality of the answer that is given to the sudden, spontaneous question.

I have come to believe that there are only five reasons in the world to open our mouths to speak.

(1) to amuse; (2) to inform; (3) to deceive; (4) to persuade; or (5) to give pleasure. All five involve thought.

(1) *Amusement.* This is absence of thought, for that is the meaning of the word *amuse*. There may be very good reason for not thinking, and we often seek the clowns of the world to help us in not doing it. There is a place for amusement in the classroom, for the mind must take a break from time to time for the same reason that the body must.

(2) *Information.* When we seek or give information, we are promoting right thinking. The information may be given in a great many different ways, and may come in different forms. This information may be simply factual, within a given framework; it may be logical information about the rules of thought or emotion; it may be an appeal to authority, or so forth.

(3) *Deception.* This is for the purpose of promoting wrong thinking.

(4) *Persuasion.* This is for the purpose of moving thought to action.

(5) *Enjoyment.* Words, written or spoken, can

give an aesthetic experience.

One of the things that characterized Jesus as the greatest of teachers was the quality of his answers to the questions that people brought. Sometimes the questions were honest, often they were designed to ensnare him, but he astonished them all with the quality of his answers (Luke 20:26).

Every question needs to be answered, even if the question is frivolous or full of guile. The wisest of all men said:

"Answer not a fool according to his folly, lest thou also be like unto him. Answer a fool according to his folly, lest he be wise in his own conceit." -- Proverbs 26:4,5

This means that we should not descend to the level of a fool in order to debate with him, but rather we should answer in such a way that his folly is revealed. Jesus did this in Matthew 21:23-27 when he exposed the duplicity of the Pharisees when they asked him if the ministry of John the Baptist was from heaven.

The teacher will not deal with the child the same way that Jesus dealt with the adult Pharisees, but it would be worthwhile for teachers to study the wisdom of his answers. Some of the things that students will remember the most about a teacher will be the answers that are given in particular situations.

Central to the giving of a good answer is understanding the question. Questions are not always what they seem. When Pilate asked Jesus if he was the King of the Jews, Jesus did not answer until he found out whether Pilate meant a king in competition with Caesar, or in the sense of the promises of God to Israel (John 18:33-37). The good teacher will always try to hear the question-- to know what the question means before answering it. So Proverbs 15:28 says "The heart of the righteous studieth to answer: but the mouth of the wicked poureth out evil things."

It is important to discern the silent question. Sometimes an appeal for information simply is that: "How do you spell Hawaii?" But it may also come from fears: "How old do you have to be to die?" Or from things at home: "Did you have any sisters?" Sometimes the question is a trap: "Mr. Jones (the Principal) said I could drop this class. Is it all right with you?" Sometimes it is a bid for sympathy: "Why do I keep failing these tests when I keep working so hard"?

Anyone who thinks that childhood is simple and innocent has simply not been around children very much or has not been aware. Teachers very often get their reputations for being unfair or harsh simply from the answers they give. They may cut students off, give curt or sarcastic answers, or dive into a matter without discerning the nature of the situation. More than anything else, the answers that teachers give seal their reputations and their effectiveness.

There is irony in this because teachers grade and promote students because of their answers, often unaware that we are being graded by them in a more important way.

"Why don't we study the Song of Solomon?" He was a high school student, a senior boy, in a Christian school Bible class who tried to have some fun at my expense. In the same spirit, I shot back, "Jack [not his real name], are you having trouble with your sexuality? Do we need to talk about this?" The class roared. After class, the young man said, "That was pretty good, Mr. Powell." It was the beginning of a good relationship between us.

The question was not an honest one, and I answered it according to its folly. I give this illustration, not as an example of unusual wisdom on my part, for I do not claim that, but as the way the Holy Spirit may often guide you. The promise of the Scripture is this: "The preparations of the heart in man, and the answer of the tongue, is from the Lord" (Proverbs 16:1).

The answer I gave might have been completely inappropriate for another student, but it fit this one perfectly. [Note: this happened in a land far away very long ago. In the modern classroom we would probably be safer to commit the lad to counseling, but it might not be so much fun or as good for the lad. It also helped that I had a good prior relationship with the boy, and knew that he would relish the attention.]

The spirit of an answer is as important, if not more important, than its content. "A soft answer turneth away wrath: but grievous words stir up anger" (Proverbs 15:1). A teacher may destroy his good counsel by the manner in which it is given. Sarcasm rarely is effective, and the wrath of man does not "work the righteousness of God" (James 1:20).

Often gentle humor and a lively imagination will open the heart and mind to truth and godliness. Good will, humility, and genuine love will guide the lips, so that our speech will always be "with grace, seasoned with salt," and we will "know how to answer every man" (Colossians 4:6).

Because the answer of the tongue is so important, we must remember the words of Christ, "A good man out of the good treasure of his heart bringeth forth that which is good; and an evil man out of the evil treasure of his heart bringeth forth that which is evil: for of the abundance of the heart his mouth speaketh" (Luke 6:45).

The secret treasure of our heart is revealed more in the answers that we give in the moment of stress than in all our prepared responses. In that moment our true character seeps out through our words and the whole world sees what we really are. The "word fitly spoken is like apples of gold in pictures of silver" (Proverbs 25:11). The treasure house of these words is the sanctified and obedient heart.

The rewards of good answers are great: "Every man shall kiss his lips that giveth a right answer" (Proverbs 24:26)
.

Chapter Five:
A City Without Walls

"He that hath no rule over his own spirit is like a city that is broken down, and without walls." --Proverbs 25:28

"He that is slow to anger is better than the mighty; and he that ruleth his spirit than he that taketh a city."
--Proverbs 16:32

"A fool's wrath is presently known: but a prudent man covereth shame." --Proverbs 12:16

"He that is slow to wrath is of great understanding: but he that is hasty of spirit exalteth folly." --Proverbs 14:29

In ancient times a city with no walls was utterly defenseless, a prey to wild animals and even wilder men. In fact, one of the first things that Israel did after returning from exile in Babylon was to rebuild the wall of Jerusalem, for a city that had no wall would soon become no city at all.

This is the figure used in Proverbs 25:28. Self-control is the wall that protects a person from the things that would destroy him.

These are days of indulgence of the spirit, not self-control. We are encouraged to "let it all hang out." No feeling is to be suppressed; no emotion is to be curbed. This often puts us in direct contradiction with Scripture.

Some admire the person who "says what he thinks," even though the Bible says "a fool uttereth all his mind: but a wise man keepeth it in till afterwards" (Proverbs 29:11). "I can't help how I feel," is the most popular excuse for everything from slander to adultery. Self-indulgence masquerades as honesty, and egoism as purpose.

The teacher who is not in control of himself has no chance of controlling the classroom.

This means control of how you feel. We certainly **can** and **must** control how we feel. Some emotions are very pleasant to us, and some of the most destructive may be the most pleasant.

Self-pity may be very entertaining and sweet to the taste. We can roll our hurts around on our tongue, savor the taste of them, and find all sorts of excuses for sinful behavior. The same is true of anger. A thrill shoots through the body as adrenaline is released and some people really enjoy the experience. Others enjoy sickness and the attention it brings; others enjoy hurt feelings.

The trouble with the self-centered person is that he is **self**-centered, not **God**-centered. His anger, his feelings, his discouragement, his self-pity are far more important to him than the glory of God and the advancement of Christian faith. He doesn't even think about how the expression of his discouragement, for instance, might cause others to be discouraged. He just indulges himself.

Self-government is government, not self-indulgence. The truly self-governed person does not need to be forced to do what is right, for he has the law of God written on his heart, and the impetus for obedience comes from within, not from without. This is the root of all free people. A slave must be whipped to obedience; a free man obeys the laws willingly.

Very few police officers are needed in a free nation where people live self-disciplined lives. When people are out of control, self-indulgent, and lawless, no amount of lawmen can keep the peace, for even the police will be lawless. The premier example of self-government in the classroom is the teacher. If he is measured, ordered, confident, and prepared, with his emotions and temper in check, the class will reflect this order. "As in water face answereth to face, so the heart of man to man." (Proverbs 27:19) Children reflect what they see. As Chaucer said, "If the gold rusts, what will the iron do?"

Chapter Six:
The Honey Is Good!

"My son, eat thou honey, because it is good; and the honeycomb, which is sweet to thy taste: So shall the knowledge of wisdom be unto thy soul: when thou hast found it, then there shall be a reward, and thy expectation shall not be cut off." --Proverbs 24:13,14

What a wonderful thing it is to know the right answer! I once knew a man who could tell what was wrong with my car just by listening to it for a few minutes. He never made a repair that was not needed. There are lawyers who can decipher the most complex legal matters, and physicians who can instantly diagnose diseases. Such people are worth whatever fee they charge.

A good teacher is that kind of person, but he deals in the very stuff of life. The whole profession of teaching rests on the assumption that the teacher knows something that the student does not know, and that this knowledge can be exchanged.

Knowledge is a crown of glory to the teacher, while ignorance is a shame. (Isaiah 62:3; Proverbs 3:35) But there is more in the verse: it is the love of knowledge that is commanded. Proverbs 2:10 says that you will be preserved when "Knowledge is pleasant unto thy soul."

Think of a great sword hanging on a wall. Underneath is a plaque that reads, "This mighty sword has won many victories in old times. It deserves our honor and respect."

Do we treat the Bible that way? Do we respect it for the past, but neglect its study and use today? There is nothing like the knowledge of the theology and practical philosophy of the Bible to prepare the teacher to teach others.

Proverbs 14:7 commands us "Go from the presence of a foolish man, when thou perceivest not in him the lips of knowledge." But what good is it to know **how** to teach, if I do not know **what** to teach. The better the methods, the more dangerous the fool.

At least two separate kinds of knowledge are essential before success in teaching can take place. The old debate about whether you teach the student or the subject is a debate over nothing. The good teacher teaches the subject to the student. Because of this, it is important to know both the subject and the student.

There is a price to pay for knowledge. That is why we are told to "Buy the truth, and sell it not; also wisdom, and instruction, and understanding" (Proverbs 23:23). The gaining of knowledge is not a painless process, but is compared to mining for treasure (Proverbs 2:3-5) usually a difficult and laborious process. But too often teachers are guilty of the very sins they condemn in their pupils: laziness, and indifference to studies. Would we dig up our front yard if we knew that priceless diamonds were buried there? There are far greater treasures in the Bible.

The good teacher will not leave studies after graduation or the mind will stagnate and leave the teacher in a rut. The mind will be dead and the teaching will be dead. The students will not be fooled. The moment a teacher ceases to love to learn is the moment he must find a new profession.

"But I do not have the time!" But if the profession that we chose is teaching, then we must give priority to our calling. The price we pay for knowledge might be less socializing, less television, a vacation spent in study. The answer we give to our students, must be given to ourselves: "You must find the time."

We must love what we teach. If we can hardly wait to get to class to teach, then the students will be excited to come. Attitudes are contagious; the teacher who hates math will impart his hatred to the class. You can change, and must change.

It is the author's firm conviction that the more you learn of a subject, the more enjoyable it will be to you. Pay the price to learn, and the fun you have will be passed on to your students.

Shame on you if you are using the same lesson plans that you used ten years ago! Has there been nothing to learn since then? Were you perfect then, and had no need to change? Your author has never used old lesson plans for this very reason. Although I have taught the same courses year after year, I have made new lesson plans each year, using the old as guides, and there is no way to describe the richness this has brought me.

I recently ran across my material for a Bible class that I taught more than fifteen years ago and was gladdened by the differences, the things I had learned. I put in new material and discard old material constantly. I do this, not for the students, but for me. Do not be afraid to change; this means that you are wiser today than you were yesterday. It is also Biblical: "If any man think that he knoweth anything, he knoweth nothing yet as he ought to know" (1 Corinthians 8:2).

Jesus put it very well, as usual: "Therefore every scribe [teacher] which is instructed unto the kingdom of heaven is like unto a man that is an householder, which bringeth forth out of his treasure things new and old" (Matthew 13:52).

What a wonderful figure! What a happy thing to

think that my mind is a treasure house that contains wonderful old antiques, as well as brand-new shiny delights!

"He that walketh with wise men shall be wise: but a companion of fools shall be destroyed" (Proverbs 13:20). There is an old Chinese story about an ancient wise man who was asked when he had been happiest. He replied, "When a young lad walked down the road, whistling, after asking me the way." Think about it.

Chapter Seven:
Building Character? Or Grinding a Fool?

"Though thou shouldest bray a fool in a mortar among wheat with a pestle, yet will not his foolishness depart from him." --Proverbs 27:22

The Bible is clear that the only way to have a good character is to be born again. The Bible states that we are born in sin (Psalm 58:3; Psalm 51:5), and that from our flesh arises no good thing (Romans 7:18).

Jesus is even more emphatic than Solomon in the figures that he uses. He said that a good tree cannot bring forth evil fruit, and a corrupt tree cannot bring forth good fruit (Matthew 7:17ff).

Paul enlarged upon this theme by saying that the flesh (the natural man) always brings forth evil fruit, and the spirit (the new man) always brings forth good fruit (Galatians 5:16-26). Jeremiah had confirmed this centuries before when he said, "Can the Ethiopian change his skin, or the leopard his spots? then may ye also do good, that are accustomed to do evil" (Jeremiah 13:23).

In short, nothing but regeneration, the new birth which the Apostle Paul calls a new creation (2 Corinthians 5:17), will produce a character that is conformable to God and to his word.

In fact, until a man is given such a new nature, his old nature is "enmity against God: for it is not subject to the law of God, neither indeed can be. So then they that are in the flesh cannot please God" (Romans 8:7,8).

It is even more emphatic, if possible, in 1 Corinthians 2:14: "For the natural man receiveth not the things of the Spirit of God: for they are foolishness unto him: neither can he know them, because they are spiritually discerned." Regeneration is the writing of God's law upon the fleshly tables of the heart, after the likeness of Christ, rather than upon the tables of stone (2 Corinthians 3:3 and Jeremiah 31:33).

In promising the new birth, God promised to "give them one heart, and I will put a new spirit within you; and I will take the stony heart out of their flesh, and will give them an heart of flesh: That they may walk in my statutes, and keep mine ordinances, and do them: and they shall be my people, and I will be their God" (Ezekiel 11:19,20).

To put it another way, there is no such thing as a neutral character, which may be developed one way or another, shaped by the environment, coerced by threat of punishment, or lifted by high ideals. This is a pagan concept and is not known in the Bible. It was popularized in the United States through the writing of John Locke and the educational philosophy of John Dewey, and has helped form the educational philosophy of modern public education.

This error also lies behind the idea of rehabilitation of the criminal through the prison system, one of humanism's most colossal failures. Unfortunately, it has had immense influence on the philosophy and character of many Christian schools.

If a godly environment with appropriate punishments and rewards, diligent administration of the laws, and separation from the rest of the world could ever have produced good character, then Israel would have been the godliest nation ever.

They were led by a pillar of fire and cloud, had the manifestation of God's own presence with them in the glory of God over the Ark of the Covenant, and were separated from the rest of the nations by God's own ordinances, statutes, and judgments. The manifestation of His presence in miracles, providences, and judgments was clearly seen.

Paul put it this way: "If righteousness come by the law, then Christ is dead in vain" (Galatians 2:21). Bible-believers know this and teach it in their churches with more or less consistency.

Salvation is in the Lord's hands. The parable of the workers in the vineyard Matthew 20 makes it clear that the time of God's call to grace is in His hand. David also confessed, "My times are in thy hand," (Psalm 31:15). Character, then, is created and then developed, not developed from Adam's flesh.

This is further indicated by the experience of the godly. Some of the godliest men of the Bible had children who were reprobate. Even Abraham, of whom it was said, "he will command his children after him...." (Genesis 18:19) had sons that were not godly: Ishmael, and the sons listed in Genesis 25. At the command of the Lord these sons were given gifts and sent from Abraham's house that Isaac might grow up free from their influence. Isaac's son Esau was ungodly, and the examples may be multiplied.

Proper discipline and chastening may be blessed of God and play a part in bringing a child to repentance and faith, according to such Scriptures as Proverbs 23:13,14, but that is another subject and beyond the scope of this chapter and this book. Others have written eloquently on this subject and it is well known to the Christian public.

What is true, however, is that the grace of God does not come by human formulas or actions, but according to God's will and purpose. Thus Israel confessed in circumcision that their hope for their children was the Spirit of God, not in the works of the flesh (Romans 4:9-13).

If the character is good, then it will ripen according to its nature. Bad character will also ripen. In the parable of the wheat and tares, Jesus tells us that as time goes along each develops according to its true nature (Matthew 13:24-30). The idea that discipline can develop "good" character that will make it "easier" for the child to become a Christian is an idea foreign to the Bible.

Generally, there are three classifications of students in the school, and membership in these classes is known only to God. **First**, there are children who have faith and know the Lord, who genuinely desire to be obedient to the Lord, but are at many levels of spiritual maturity. **Second**, there are children who will believe, but as yet have not come to faith and do not know the Lord. They are like Samuel serving in the tabernacle (1 Samuel 3:7). They may be from Christian homes, may know much of the language of Christianity, and may "approve that which is good" (Romans 2:18-21), and may be able to answer most questions in their Bible classes. **Third**, there are children who will prove to be reprobate, as Esau, and will never come to the faith. In outward behavior, it is impossible for us to tell the difference between these classifications.

We should not be surprised at these classifications, for Jesus had those same classifications among his own disciples. There were those who were "Israelites indeed," such as Nathaniel (John 1:47). Then there were those among the twelve who did not yet believe (John 6:64). There were also those who would prove to be reprobate as Judas, who was a devil from the beginning (John 6:70). If this was the condition of the adults who followed Jesus, how much more shall we expect to see these same conditions among children in a school? We find the same classifications of people in Israel as a whole when Jesus came.

The implications for the school are significant. A system of discipline and rules is necessary in order to keep order and to maintain our Christian witness; if it is Biblical and administered with grace, this system may be blessed of God; repentance and faith may follow. We deceive ourselves, however, if we think that the multiplying of rules, especially man-made rules, will "build character." This puts a burden upon human laws and rules that they cannot bear.

This is the meaning of Ephesians 6:4. As Matthew Henry puts it: "Do not provoke your children to wrath. Your children are pieces of yourselves, and therefore ought to be governed with great tenderness and love. When you caution them, when you counsel them, when you reprove them, do it in such a manner as not to provoke them to wrath, endeavoring to convince their judgments and to work upon their reason." Certainly it is the sinful nature of the child that is provoked to wrath, for wrath is a work of the flesh (Galatians 5:20). This is exactly the point.

Parents and teachers must behave in such a way that the flesh is not provoked and inflamed. The flesh is not changed by provoking; it is slain by the death of Jesus Christ so that those called of God may become new in Christ (2 Corinthians 5:14-17).

It is the inward man that must be reached, and he can only be reached by the power of the Word of God, energized by the Holy Spirit. Rigidity and overdependence upon rules and regulations will bring anger and rejection in those that have not yet come to faith, and will harden the heart against the truth. This is not building character, but inciting revolution. When you abrade a fool, you do not create peace, but bring your own judgment into question; and be assured, that little child you love so much, is a fool until he is born again.

The theme of the book of Galatians is to this point. The Galatians supposed that keeping the rules and regulations of the old covenant would perfect them as Christians (Galatians 3:3). Paul said that this is a deceptive dream, that the Christian character is the work of the Spirit and there can never be any peace between those who are born of the flesh and those who are born of the Spirit (Galatians 4:28, 29). Dependence upon rules and regulations to produce good character is confidence in the flesh, and by this confidence the flesh gains power. We are not to be deceived:

"Be not deceived; God is not mocked: for whatsoever a man soweth, that shall he also reap. For he that soweth to his flesh shall of the flesh reap corruption; but he that soweth to the Spirit shall of the Spirit reap life everlasting." --Galatians 6:7,8

This is the reason Paul said that the true Israel of God are those who "have no confidence in the flesh" (Philippians 3:3). In other words, this dependence is not going to produce what you think it will produce. You think that you are going to get good Christian character; instead, you will get "adultery, fornication, uncleanness, lasciviousness, idolatry, witchcraft, hatred, variance, emulations, wrath, strife, seditions, heresies, envyings, murders, drunkenness, revelings, and such like" (Galatians 5:19-21).

But there is more. Young people who do believe will also have the flesh aroused by this false philosophy. You may see two responses: some Christian young people may be pushed into rebellion (The flesh produces the same thing, whether in a Christian or in a non-Christian. There is no hope for the flesh; this is why Jesus died. See Galatians 5:16-21 and James 4:5 with context); other Christian young people may be tempted into spiritual pride and hypocrisy.

It is far easier to keep rules and regulations outwardly than it is to take up your cross and follow Jesus Christ. The first can be of the flesh; the second is the work of the Spirit alone.

Paul was a proud Pharisee and fancied that he was blameless before the law, until "the law came" [truly taught him by Jesus Christ and His Spirit] and then he died. (Romans 7:9). It was that tenth commandment that had to do with the inward man that got him and destroyed his self-confidence and Phariseeism.

David said, "The law of the Lord is perfect, converting the soul" (Psalm 19:7). God's law certainly plays a critical role in the transformation of character, for it reveals the true nature of our sin and drives us to Jesus Christ (Galatians 3:24).

Therefore, the Ten Commandments must be taught and their outward applications enforced, for crimes against the school and its citizens must not be tolerated. When violations of the Ten Commandments such as swearing, lying, and stealing occur, we have a wonderful opportunity to instruct children as to the nature of sin and the importance of repentance and faith, but the multiplying of man-made rules for any other purposes than the keeping of order or for Christian testimony is wrong, and promotes rebellion and hypocrisy.

It is said, "Do not try to teach a pig to talk. You will not succeed, and will only irritate the pig."

Chapter Eight:
Finding the Idea Ox

"Where no oxen are, the crib is clean: but much increase is by the strength of the ox." --Proverbs 14:4

The Bible recognizes that there is no perfection in this world, and very often there must be a tradeoff. A clean barn is desirable, but not at the expense of the work of the ox.

If you want to enjoy the use and blessing of an ox, you have to shovel some manure. The best Christians have things wrong with them. In Romans 7:21, the Apostle Paul admitted that "when I would do good, evil is present with me." Gifts are given by God according to His purpose (1 Corinthians 12:6ff), and every gift has a downside. God called David to be a man of war, to kill Philistines and consolidate the nation of Israel. Hence, he was unfit to build the temple at Jerusalem (1 Chronicles 28:3,4).

A person can do a great deal of evil if he is squeamish about the mess in the crib. The man with one talent hid it in the ground because he was afraid he would get in trouble for not using it to perfection (Matthew 25). In a vain longing after perfection, many people fritter away their whole lives doing nothing for fear of messing up their clean stable. Every great man who ever lived, in the church or state, had people who carped and complained because he was not perfect enough to suit their tastes.

This author has taught in Christian schools for all of his adult life, and has lived long enough to see how some of the young people have apparently turned out. I have learned that it is nearly impossible to tell what a kid is truly made of by observing him in school, even in high school. Some students who cause trouble are hard to teach, because they have confidence in their opinions and desires.

Those who teach them must be prepared to shovel a lot, but the strength of the ox is there and they will accomplish much in God's kingdom. On the other hand, some students may cause no trouble because they lack confidence and simply desire to please.

This does not mean that we approve of manure. By no means. It simply means that we are realists, and recognize that no men are perfect; all have faults and failures. It also means that we recognize that we can obtain a clean barn in only two ways: by getting rid of the oxen and getting nothing done; or by doing a lot of shoveling. It is possible to imagine an ideal ox that works hard, eats very little, and makes his mess in the compost pile. One thing only is wrong with our image: that ox does not exist and will not exist. Wisdom and maturity teach us to separate our dreams from reality.

It is unfortunate that some modern translations miss the point of this verse. The word "clean" does not mean "empty" in any other place that it is used in the Bible. In Job 11:4 it stands for doctrine that is "clean" or pure in God's sight; in Psalm 73:1 it is used of a "clean" heart; in Psalm 19:8 the commandments of the Lord are "pure"; the loved one of the Song of Solomon 6:9 is "choice." In this place to say the "manger is empty" is to take a secondary meaning, and to miss the main teaching of the verse.

On this verse the great expositor Matthew Henry says, "Where no oxen are, to till the ground and tread out the corn, the crib is empty, is clean; there is no straw for the cattle, and consequently no bread for the service of man. The crib indeed is clean from dung, which pleases the neat and nice, that cannot endure husbandry because there is so much dirty work in it, and therefore will sell their oxen to keep the crib clean."

The rejection of the ox because it makes a mess stems from a wrong set of values, the inability to discern between what is important and what is of lesser importance. The Pharisees could not tell a gnat from a camel, or a mote from a two-by-four. It is not fun to have a gnat in your throat, but a wise man knows it is not a camel. A mote in the eye may feel like a two-by-four, unless you have had a two-by-four in your eye; then you might know the difference.

Having no valid rule of measure to distinguish between great and little things, the Pharisees had no judgment, and what was worse, they thought God was as trivial as they were. You can almost hear them say, "Well, sin is sin," leaving the impression that they had a more finely-tuned sense of sin than lesser mortals. They did not understand when Jesus said for them to pay more attention to the "weightier matters' of the law (Matthew 23:23).

It is true that men before God are either justified in Christ or are yet in their sins and rebellion. But a child of God does not sin as an unbeliever does (Deuteronomy 32:5), and even the sins of unbelievers are not all equal. Sins are not all equal in God's eyes, and must not be in ours, for wise men must discern between gnats and camels. The effect of equalizing all sins will not make us abhor small sins, but will make us trivialize great ones. We strain at gnats and swallow camels.

It is especially important in the classroom to be able to recognize what is important and what is not important. Why is that child so rowdy? Is it because he has been called of God someday to contend with Goliath? We would not expect him to behave as one called to a life of quiet scholarship. The strength of the ox may be there, and require our special attention. More work? Of course! Also more patience and wisdom.

Related to this idea is the Biblical concept of love. True love does not exist in the abstract. 1 John 4:20 warns about this: "If a man say, I love God, and hateth his brother, he is a liar: for he that loveth not his brother who he hath seen, how can he love God whom he hath not seen?" Such abstract love is just a flutter in the mind. It was said of a great public figure once, "He is a great humanitarian in the abstract; he just can't stand people." Also, almost every church has members who agonize over foreign "heathen," but who are not nice to their relatives.

A friend of mine has a favorite proverb that cuts across conventional wisdom: "Anything worth doing, is worth doing badly." It would be nice if the ox did not mess up the stable, but God did not make him that way. God did not make us or our children that way either, and if we wait for perfection, nothing will get done. Should we strive for perfection? Absolutely. But we must not wait for it.

A related idea is in Ecclesiastes 1:15 and 7:13:

"That which is crooked cannot be made straight: and that which is wanting cannot be numbered.... Consider the work of God: for who can make that straight, which he hath made crooked."

God has filled the world with crooked places and things which are lacking. This is to teach us to prepare for heaven (Ecclesiastes 7:14). A misplaced idealism has pulled many a young person into the teaching field, only to bring about his professional ruin as his idealism leads him into conflict with his peers, his administration, and even with the parents of the children he is hired to serve. Look at the greatest preachers of the past and present, and you will find crooked places that could not be made straight, and things wanting that could not be numbered. This is what heaven is for, where the crooked will be made straight, and the rough places smooth. We are not there yet.

There is wisdom here somewhere: God made the ox. The ox messes up the crib. We need the ox in order to get the work done. Being too good to clean the crib will mean that no work will get done. Think of that!

As usual, there is a passage in the Bible that says all this very neatly:

"Be not righteous overmuch: neither make thyself

over wise: why shouldest thou destroy thyself? Be not over much wicked, neither be thou foolish: why shouldest thou die before thy time (Ecclesiastes 7:16,17)?

As Matthew Henry puts it: "Be not opinionative, and conceited of thy own abilities. Set not up for a critic, to find fault with everything that is said and done." A man that is too good to shovel the crib, who finds dirt everywhere and pretends great horror at it, is worth nothing for this earth and is too hypocritical for the next.

There is an old story about the drunk who went to sleep on the park bench. A couple of youths came along and thought to have fun with him by rubbing limburger cheese into this mustache. They watched him for a while, became bored and wandered off.

The old drunk awoke after a while and sniffed the air around him and swore under his breath. He walked across the lawn to the sidewalk, picked a flower, put it to his nose and then cast it aside with disgust.

Walking down the sidewalk he snorted as a young pretty girl walked by and wondered aloud about her perfume. She ignored him.

Entering his favorite bar, he took his place on the bar stool and ordered his favorite drink. The bartender poured it and slid it down the bar to him. The drunk took one smell of it and set it aside.

"Ain't it awful?" he said to the bartender.

"What's awful?" the bartender asked in return.

"Well, the whole world smells rotten."

He was smelling his own smell everywhere he went, and thought it was the world that smelled. If you think the whole world stinks, check under your own nose.

Thus it is with those who cannot find enough purity anywhere to suit them.

13 Who is a wise man and endued with knowledge among you? let him shew out of a good conversation his works with meekness of wisdom.
14 But if ye have bitter envying and strife in your hearts, glory not, and lie not against the truth.
15 This wisdom descendeth not from above, but is earthly, sensual, devilish.
16 For where envying and strife is, there is confusion and every evil work.
17 But the wisdom that is from above is first pure, then peaceable, gentle, and easy to be intreated, full of mercy and good fruits, without partiality, and without hypocrisy.
18 And the fruit of righteousness is sown in peace of them that make peace. –James 4:13-18

Chapter Nine
Jesus is Savior, So Don't Meddle

"He that passeth by, and meddleth with strife belonging not to him, is like one that taketh a dog by the ears." --Proverbs 26:17

"It is an honor for a man to cease from strife: but every fool will be meddling." --Proverbs 20:3

Jesus said that we will be blessed if we suffer for righteousness sake. Peter not only repeats the promise, but puts a caution with it:

"If ye be reproached for the name of Christ, happy are ye; for the spirit of glory and of God resteth upon you: on their part he is evil spoken of, but on your part he is glorified. But let none of you suffer as a murderer, or as a thief, or as an evildoer, or as a busybody in other men's matters" (1 Peter 4:14, 15).

It is interesting that the great Apostle included "busybodies" in the same list with murderers, thieves, and evildoers. Being a meddler and being righteous are not the same thing.

In the view of the author, teaching is one of the noblest and most rewarding occupations on the earth. Very few people have so many opportunities to do so much good for so many people as does the schoolteacher. It is also true, that very few people have as many opportunities to meddle in other people's business.

Some schools are organized under the philosophy that the school stands in the place of the parents. Others look on the school as the ministry of a particular church. Still others believe that the school is a private educational institution built upon Christian principles. Whatever the organizing philosophy, Christian people everywhere believe that the primary responsibility for educational decisions rests with the parents.

It is easy for the school to develop a messianic dream. Many of us fell into the trap almost without thinking. The spirit of the age so much affects us that its philosophy crept in through our very pores. Public education grew up in America with a messianic dream. Whatever ills we faced as a nation we had confidence that proper education would cure them. We expended huge sums of money on education, and probably no nation in history has experimented with so many different concepts of education, or expected so much from our schools.

As a result, the schools of America have become a major battle-ground as special-interest groups seek to use them to advance their programs, whether it be for social peace, sex education, drug abuse programs, driving education, transcendental meditation, vegetarianism, radical feminism, homosexuality, same-sex marriage, or comparative religion.

If the school is to be our savior, then it must be given the power and means to do this. Because of court decisions removing the Christian faith from public schools, the public schools have more and more come to be dominated by those driven by a humanistic dream.

When your author was a little boy attending Wednesday night prayer meetings in our little country church in southern Oregon, I heard godly men and women pray time and time again for revival to come to America. I joined my voice in that prayer many times.

In some ways the revival came, but not in the way we had expected. It came in a way that even the humanistic establishment could not have imagined. No one could have predicted that Bible-believers would have peacefully paid their taxes to support public education, and at the same time would have spent billions of dollars to erect an alternate school system where the Bible and traditional Christian and family values are taught. The long-term effect of this revival of religion is yet to be known.

The messianic dream, however, did not go away,

but moved with us into the Christian school. Do our children suffer from a bad environment in public school? **We** will save them by putting them into the good environment of a Christian school. What public school tried to do, we will do better in the Christian school.

The Bible teaches us that there is only one Savior, Jesus Christ, our risen and reigning Lord. Any state, school, or church, that pretends to be the salvation for men lies under the curse of God, for Christ is the only "name under heaven, whereby we must be saved" (Acts 4:12).

There's the rub, as Hamlet said. Because Christ is our Lord, he has power and authority to be our Savior. It is not meddling when he works in us both "to will and to do of his good pleasure" (Philippians 2:13). Not so for the self-appointed savior. The messianic dream manifests itself in incessant meddling in other people's affairs. The self-appointed savior, whether individual or institution, professes to know what is best for every family and seeks to intrude into every area of life. The secular state, as it assumes a messianic role, meddles more and more into the daily affairs of its citizens.

I remember how angry my mother was one day when she was told by an arrogant public school official, "We have been educated and we are the experts. We know what is best for your child." This is the mindset of the official in the messianic institution, one who believes that he is justified in his meddling, because his institution is the hope and salvation of the world.

A contractual relationship exists between a family and the Christian school. It may be stated in various ways, but the school concentrates capital and divides labor in order to carry on education in an efficient and cost-effective way. The school-teacher is employed to provide a certain definite service.

If I hire a roofer to come fix my leaking roof, I do not expect him to monkey around trying to tune my piano. In the same way, I do not expect the math teacher in my Christian school to instruct me on what time my children should be in bed, or what they should eat for breakfast. He is hired to teach the quadratic equation and the definite integral.

The average Christian parent does not enroll his children in the Christian school because he thinks he needs to be instructed in child-rearing, child discipline, or even theology. He may be wrong, but he is wrong before his own master, Jesus Christ. He is not accountable to the school or to the Christian teacher.

He wants his child to learn reading, writing, arithmetic, and the other disciplines within the framework of the Scripture. He wants his child to learn the Bible. He did not, however, employ the teacher to meddle in his home.

The Holy Spirit warns us about this particular mind set in James 3:1: "My brethren, be not many masters, knowing that we shall receive the greater condemnation." The word "master" simply means "teacher," and is used by Jesus of Himself in Matthew 23:8. The remainder of James 3 warns us of the evils the tongue can do when we become instructive and meddlesome in other people's affairs.

The truly wise man, according to James, will manifest the "meekness of wisdom," and will not be filled with "bitter envying and strife" (James 3:13). The wisdom that is from above is "pure, peaceable, gentle, east to be entreated, full of mercy and good fruits, without partiality, and without hypocrisy" (James 3:17).

It is a common temptation for each of us to think that our particular ministry is the most important one. Thus, those who serve in foreign missions may think that their mission is the most important one. Those who labor in Christian school may fall also into the same temptation. For this same reason strife may develop between church-run schools and the church that sponsors them.

The simple truth is that the world will not be saved through our particular ministry. The Kingdom of God is very broad and covers a multitude of ministries and duties. In the providence of God, each of them has its responsibilities and labors. The vision that drives the foreign missionary is different from the one that drives the Christian school teacher, and each of these is different from the one that drives those who run homes for unwed mothers. Each of us is but a co-worker together with Christ, who is the only Savior.

What happens if people are messing things up, and not doing right? What if Johnny comes to school with only a cup of hot chocolate for breakfast? As Christian teachers we must learn to respond in the same way that any Christian must respond when he sees his brother err. Paul gives the requirements in Romans 15:14, "I myself also am persuaded of you, my brethren, that ye also are full of goodness, filled with all knowledge, able also to admonish one another."

Being filled with goodness, I must learn to forbear and to forgive (Colossians 3:13); I must learn to justify my neighbor (Proverbs 17:15), and try to see his side of the matter; I must try to be a helper to his joy, not a lord and master over him (2 Corinthians 1:24); I also must consider my own faults and failures (Galatians 6:1), and seek to remove any beam from my own eye so I can see clearly to help him.

The Christian school teacher is put at the very heart of the Christian family, with the family's most precious possession in his care for several hours of the day. There is no place that requires greater wisdom and delicacy, humility and faithfulness. The teacher who shows humility and good sense, who always upholds and respects the authority and privilege of the family will be honored and loved by the families, and will do them immense good.

We are familiar with the words of Christ, "Whosoever will be chief among you, let him be your servant: Even as the Son of man came not to be ministered unto, but to minister, and to give his life a ransom for many" (Matthew 20:27,28).

We hold it to be fundamental to the concept of a Christian home, that children are given to families, not to churches, schools, or to states. The careful teacher will not meddle, but will perform his job as a sacred trust. The Apostle Paul put it another way: "Who art thou that judgest another man's servant? to his own master he standeth or falleth. Yea, he shall be holden up, for God is able to make him stand" (Romans 14:4).

Chapter Ten
The Piercings of a Sword

"There are many devices in a man's heart; nevertheless the counsel of the Lord, that shall stand." --Proverbs 19:21
"There is that speaketh like the piercings of a sword: but the tongue of the wise is health." --Proverbs 12:18

We all know the difference words can make. Some words go to the heart of the child and transform him. Such words are described in Hebrews 4:12:

"The word of God is quick, and powerful, and sharper than any twoedged sword, piercing even to the dividing asunder of soul and spirit, and of the joints and marrow, and is a discerner of the thoughts and intents of the heart."

Other words are like the piercing of a sword, but they leave bitterness behind. What are the differences between the Sword of the Spirit that gives health and strength, and those bitter piercings that produce sorrow and bitterness? Much of it has to do with the integrity and privacy of the individual.

One day Samuel the prophet went to Bethlehem to anoint a king for Israel. Samuel offered a sacrifice to the Lord, and the sons of Jesse were brought before Samuel. Samuel looked at Eliab, the eldest and said to himself, "This is surely the Lord's anointed." We should never forget God's words to Samuel on that occasion:

"Look not on his countenance, or on the height of his stature; because I have refused him: for the Lord seeth not as man seeth; for man looketh on the outward appearance, but God looketh on the heart" (1 Samuel 16:7).

No teacher can know what is in the heart of a child. Sometimes we may get a glimpse, for actions and words spring from the depths of the heart, but only God knows the heart.

A common sin of those in authority, whether parents, teachers, or ministers is to presume to know what is in the heart. Motives are assigned and devices are guessed at which only God can discover. The word "devices" in Proverbs 19:21 comes from a word which means something "woven together" or "textured."

It can also mean a "machine," something complicated, working together. The center of a person is made of such "weavings" of motives, desires, pretenses, hopes, fears, and beliefs that only God can sort it all out. We cannot even know our own hearts, and those that trust in their own hearts are "fools" (Proverbs 28:26).

The Lord Jesus, as always, is the best example of what teaching ought to be. Jesus always predicated his teaching upon the premise that those who heard stood in direct contact with the God Who made them. His teaching, therefore, always assumed that the hearer was either in tune with God, or in rebellion against Him.

If the hearer was in tune with God, then everything did not need to be explained, and the privacy of the person did not need to be violated. On the other hand, if the person was in rebellion to God, nothing external would convince him. This is the meaning of the phrase used so often by Christ, "He that hath ears to hear, let him hear" (Matthew 13:9 and others). This also explains why he spoke in parables (Matthew 13:10-13).

Those who presume to know what is in the heart of a child, and speak accordingly, may do much damage. In the view of this writer, much of secular modern psychology is based upon this very wrong presumption: that it is possible to know the heart. The result is self-deception, and what is worse, the confirmation of the sinner in his own self-deception. Building upon this false foundation, practitioners of this pseudo-science have told the modern age that alcoholism is sickness, homosexuality is inborn, and religion is emotion. By God's grace, Christians like Jay Adams and others are exerting a powerful corrective, but the damage to the modern age has been great.

The teacher who really believes that he cannot know the hearts of his students will approach his class with a greater dependency upon prayer, the Scriptures, and the Holy Spirit.

How piercing are those words which presume to know the heart! "You are just trying to get attention!" "Quit trying to show off!" "You must not be a Christian." "Do you think you are above the law!" "Are you better than everybody else?" Most readers will remember such from their own childhood and schooldays. They go to the heart and fester like sores, and cause pain when they are remembered years later, even in adulthood.

My heart, your heart, and heart of a child are very private places, made for fellowship with God. The inmost heart is a sanctuary that is formed for the presence of God Himself. To violate this sanctuary is to violate the very personhood of the child. When we do this the results are uniformly evil: either there is resentment as the child tries to keep something of himself or there is a loss of himself as he accepts our view of himself.

In the first case, we teachers often exacerbate the condition by preaching about "submission to authority," and being "humble," not even realizing that we have committed the most terrible of pride's offenses by usurping the very prerogative of God Himself to approach the sanctuary of the heart. In the second case, we may likewise re-enforce the loss of identity by praising a child for his conformity.

The end result of the first case is very often a turning away from the church, for the focus has been changed from submission to Christ to submission to churchly authorities. The end result of the second case is a cold and dead membership that has much outward conformity, but little true spiritual life. These patterns may be set very early.

At the core of the Protestant Reformation was the evangelical doctrine of the priesthood of the believer. The medieval church had taught that the soul could approach God only through the sacraments of the church, and these could only be administered by a lawfully ordained priest.

The evangelical doctrine was that each soul stood in direct contact with his Creator, either as a believing covenant keeper or as a unbelieving covenant breaker. Each man was responsible, therefore, to know the Scripture, believe the gospel, and bring his life into conformity to the will of God. This was his liberty and his responsibility.

Individual responsibility brings with it the risks of failure, of great diversity, but also the possibility of great individual holiness and achievement.

It was this doctrine of the priesthood of the believer that transformed the church. It required the translation of the Bible into the language of the people. Because preaching was restored, even the architecture of the church was changed, for the pulpit replaced the altar of the medieval church.

The ministry was seen as the gift of Jesus Christ to the church to edify and build up the people in their knowledge of the Scriptures, so they could make mature free choices as God's responsible children, and not follow blindly the dictates of human authorities (Ephesians 4:8-16). They were to be the Lord's freemen (1 Corinthians 7:22).

What does this have to do with the classroom teacher? A great deal. The teacher must see himself as a helper to the faith of the children. He must respect that altar that makes up the core of each child's being, each person's being. He must not presume to know the thoughts and intents of the heart, for this belongs to God alone.

Wrong actions and words, wrong ideas that are expressed, and wrong tendencies certainly must be corrected by the standard of Scripture, but the teaching of the Scripture concerning individual responsibility before the Lord must be taught and practiced, the dignity of each child held inviolate.

Dictatorial societies, whether of home, school, or state, produce only two kinds of citizens: slaves and rebels, for there can be no middle ground. The Protestant emphasis on individual responsibility brought about the greatest explosion of liberty in the history of the world, as people took upon themselves the responsibility to be just and holy in their actions, to provide for themselves economically, to build churches, schools, and benevolent societies.

The Christian school movement in America in the last decades has been the result of this kind of responsibility. It has had no leader, no central funding, no set of regulations or order. It has had sad abuses, but outstanding triumphs. It is significant that as the secular state has assumed more power during this same time, taking responsibility for more and more of the lives of Americans, we have seen the increase in numbers of people who must be cared for, and more and more people who rebel.

There is much made today of the "right of privacy." It has even been used to justify abortion, and forms the foundation of Roe vs. Wade, the Supreme Court decision that legalized abortion in the United States. But true privacy begins in the worship between a man and his God. This is why Jesus said:

"When thou prayest, thou shalt not be as the hypocrites are: for they love to pray standing in the synagogue and in the corners of the streets, that they may be seen of men. Verily I say unto you, They have their reward. But thou, when thou prayest, enter into thy closet, and when thou hast shut thy door, pray to thy father which is in secret; and thy Father which seeth in secret shall reward thee openly" (Matthew 6:5,6).

A student of mine attended a "spiritual life" conference at his church, which got him all pumped up spiritually. He came to see me, bubbling with enthusiasm. We stood on my front lawn (I was raking the grass) as he told me about the wonderful spiritual experience of the conference.

Then he said, "How much time do you spend in prayer every day?" Remembering his youth and the many follies of my own youth, I tried to avoid the question, but he persisted, saying that the speakers at the conference had urged participants to use this approach to promote "spirituality" in their community.

Finally, as gently as I could I told him that it was none of his affair, referring to Matthew 6:5,6. In this I followed the example of Christ in John 21:22. I was not as effective as Christ, however, and the young man went off convinced that I was not a spiritual as I should be. He was right about that part, of course.

This is too much the spirit of the age, I am afraid. To be healthy psychologically we must let it all "hang out." We must bore all our companions with the most intimate details of our walk with the Lord. Silence, which used to be golden, is now a sign of withdrawal and lack of self-confidence.

We are urged to let our rage, our hate, our emotion spill out at the slightest cause, lest its evil acid destroy our souls, no matter how much damage it does to those around us, or how much it bores them. We do this because we must be "in touch" with our emotions.

In forgetting to defend that most private altar upon which we offer incense most precious to God, we will find that all other precious privacies will be taken from us. Those who seek to usurp that most precious place of freedom and responsibility will leave us very little other privacy.

"Withdraw thy foot from thy neighbor's house; lest he be weary of thee, and so hate thee."
--Proverbs 25:17

Chapter Eleven:
Honor to Whom Honor Is Due

"Withhold not good from them to whom it is due, when it
is in the power of thine hand to do it. Say not unto thy
neighbor, Go, and come again, and tomorrow I will give;
when thou hast it by thee."
--Proverbs 3:27,28

Paul tells us that the fulfilling of the law is to "owe
no man anything, but to love one another: for he
that loveth another hath fulfilled the law" (Romans
13:8). There is both a negative and a positive side
to love.

Negatively, true love means that we do not do any
kind of evil to our neighbor (Romans 13:10).
Positively, we are to "do good unto all men,
especially unto them who are of the household of
faith" (Galatians 6:10).

Very few Christian teachers fail to love their
students in the negative sense: they do not abuse
their students in any way. But very often
Christians fail to see the positive requirements of
love. This principle is expressed in such passages
as following:

"Therefore to him that knoweth to do good, and
doeth it not, to him it is sin." --James 4:17
"Render therefore to all their dues: tribute to whom

tribute is due; custom to whom custom; fear to whom fear; honor to whom honor." --Romans 13:7

"Honor to whom honor is due." This writer has known teachers who were grudging with compliments and praise because they were afraid of "puffing up" a student. There are several things wrong with this attitude, in the opinion of this writer.

First, it usurps the place of God Himself. "God resisteth the proud" (1 Peter 5:5). Second, it presumes to judge that which cannot be known, except by God Himself. Only God knows the heart. Third, it is disobedient to the express commandment to give honor to whom honor is due, and many other like commandments.

Every person is to be honored for the gifts that God has given him. Although Romans 13:7 speaks primarily to rulers, yet the general principle applies. God is the author of every good gift (James 1:17), and He is honored when we honor His gifts. Does a student have good penmanship? Let us honor him for it; at the same time try to teach him to give God glory for it. Does a student excel in athletics (we usually are not remiss in these honors!)? Does she sing beautifully? What about the student who takes shy and backward students under her wing, to help them cope with school?

Psychologists have identified several types of intelligence. Usually only two types were emphasized much in the Christian school: verbal and mathematical. This is true because the Christian school movement was yet in its infancy and verbal and mathematical programs were cheaper than other programs. Then, most Christian schools are geared to college entrance programs and only verbal and math skills are tested on college entrance examinations.

Because of this, innate ability in mechanics, aesthetics, "people" skills, music, and others are often neglected. Parents and teachers must be wise to see these abilities and give praise and encouragement when possible. Parents can and should provide other opportunities for children in the summer, in church, or in other non-school activities. In this way, we may find other ways to the heart and mind of the student who struggles with the "regular" curriculum. Encouragement in other areas will very often improve a student's performance in these "regular" areas.

The Apostle Paul was careful to begin all his epistles with praise to the churches. Even the Corinthian church that had so many problems with divisions, heresies, immorality, and other things were complimented: "for the grace of God which is given you by Jesus Christ; that in everything ye are enriched by him, in all utterance, and in all knowledge..." (1 Corinthians 1:4,5).

Because we have been created in the image of God, we have a desire and need for recognition and praise. Solomon said that "A good name is rather to be chosen than great riches, and loving favor rather than silver and gold (Proverbs 22:1)." Negatively, the Ninth Commandment forbids us to bear false witness against our neighbor, for this is destructive to his reputation, and may bring all sorts of harm to him.

Jesus said that the man who used his talents wisely would be complimented and given a reward (Matthew 25:14-30).

The sin of pride is the desire to usurp the place of God. Thus, Satan tempted Eve to eat of the fruit, "to be like God," that is, to be an original, deciding for herself what was good and evil. It was not wrong for Eve to want to be "like God" in a creaturely sense, listening to his word, following his commandments. God himself would glorify her for that.

Very often the cure for students seeking attention wrongly is to give them the legitimate attention and praise that they deserve. If the teacher has eyes to see there will be many, many opportunities through the day to praise and honor students.

I once knew a teacher who kept a notebook with each student's name, and would record the day that she gave the student a compliment. She tried to never let a week go by without praising each student at least once. Need I also say that she was a most effective and beloved teacher? She also recognized that she had to be disciplined in this grace also, or some student would slip through the cracks and not receive deserved recognition.

One of the most important goals of a quality education is to help students develop the gifts that God has given them. Some students are slow to "blossom out." Because of this, they flounder around and may be hard to teach or motivate. A teacher will often fall into nagging and criticism, to the detriment of both the student and the teacher.

Many years ago I missed a great opportunity to help such a student. He broke the rules of our school by using marijuana. The rules of the school were clear and we enforced them, expelling the young man from school. We were involved in a building program at that time, and the young man donated his time for the next several months, working on the construction. He worked hard, and was readmitted the next semester.

At the end of the school year, I acknowledge

everyone who had donated time or money for the new building, but I failed to honor this student. I had many excuses in my mind for not doing it: not wishing to embarrass his parents further, not willing to call attention to a bad time in this young man's life, my busy schedule, etc.

But all these should have been overshadowed by the extraordinary grace given to him. We have since talked about this, and it is right between us, but I do not think of it without a twinge. Since that time, the young man has finished college and seminary, and I have served on the examination committee for his ordination to the gospel ministry.

Some schools will withhold awards from those who are not deemed "spiritual." The result: instead of stirring students to be "spiritual," students become more rebellious and resent the "spiritual" kids. Usually, "spiritual" in this sense means conformity to the expectations of the faculty, instead of developing and using gifts for the service of God.

There are very few things that will produce rebellion and discord more than trying to "humble" students, and "put them in their place." Students will instinctively resent and resist. Like begets like. The pride that causes a teacher to do this will simply inflame the pride of the student and do

Chapter Twelve:
Stirring Up Strife

"A talebearer revealeth secrets: but he that is of a faithful
spirit concealeth the matter."   --Proverbs 11:13
"Debate thy cause with thy neighbor himself; and discover
not a secret to another...."   --Proverbs 25:9
"He that covereth a transgression seeketh love; but he that
repeateth a matter separateth very friends." --Proverbs 17:9
"Hatred stirreth up strifes: but love covereth all sins." --
Proverbs 10:12

"Jack is so lazy, he just won't do anything!" "I can't stand that kid; he is such a smart-aleck." "Judy just thinks she doesn't have to keep the rules."

Teachers sometimes forget that students are people, too, and are to be treated the same way as other Christians. This means that it is wrong to slander them, to discuss their faults, or to otherwise damage their reputations.

This is one reason I avoided teachers' lounges. It is not because I was anti-social or possess a higher degree of wisdom or virtue than others: just the opposite. The lounge offers too much of a temptation for me to commit the sins described above. I have been guilty too many times to think I am immune.

We are commanded in Colossians 3:11-15 to "put on...bowels of mercies, kindness, humbleness of mind, meekness, longsuffering: forbearing one another, and forgiving one another, if any man have a quarrel against any: even as Christ forgave you, so also do ye. And above all these things put on charity, which is the bond of perfectness. And let the peace of God rule in your hearts...."

So also in Ephesians 4:31,32: "Let all bitterness, and wrath, and anger, and clamor, and evil speaking, be put away from you, will all malice; And be ye kind one to another...."

It is too bad if an "us against them" attitude develops in the student body. This attitude will always be present to a certain extent among junior and senior high students, because of the natural rebelliousness of youth, but certain things can be avoided that often cause the condition to worsen: among the most important are destructive conversations among the teachers concerning the students.

We deceive ourselves if we think that the students do not know. Students overhear conversations; children of faculty members say things; we give ourselves away in a thousand ways. Sometimes teachers will use expressions that other teachers have used about a student, tipping their hand.

Students have sensitive antennae that let them know when teachers have an "attitude" about them. "My teacher doesn't like me," they tell their parents.

Our attitude toward people (and our students) is influenced to a large extent by what others have said about them. This is the reason for the Ninth Commandment. For this reason, I make it a regular practice not to consult the cumulative records of a student for anything but health data before a school year, because I do not think it fair for a student to begin a school year with all the baggage of previous years hanging over him.

Even the Lord's mercies are new every day (Lamentations 2:22,23)! We ought to allow a student a fresh start every year. For the same reason I have made it a practice over the years not to include behavioral matters in the cumulative record, for I believe that such a "dossier" is contrary to Scripture. Most of us would object strenuously to such a record being kept anywhere on us as adults; they can serve no good purpose for students.

When 1 Corinthians 13:5 says that love "thinketh no evil," the word for "think" is a term used also to mean "reckon up an account." Love does not keep accounts of all the evil done. In fact, as a principal I made it a personal practice for years to remove negative behavioral reports from the records.

Is the student "lazy"? This is another way of saying that he is not motivated. This is a challenge to the teacher, not a reason for complaining about the student. Does the student engage in wrong behavior? Once again, this is not a reason for complaining about him, but a time to follow clearly defined biblical procedures. He is to be confronted with his sin; consultations must be taken with his parents; proper disciplinary action is to be taken.

If the behavior does not warrant disciplinary action, then we are to forbear in mercy. In any case, backbiting or slander is not a professional nor a Christian response.

This Biblical prohibition about slander and backbiting is well known in Christian circles, as are the evil results that proceed from them. The lessons that we try to teach in our Bible classes must be learned in our own hearts; slander and evil speaking proceed from sin in the heart. It is hatred that stirs up strife, but love covers all sins.

As Charles Bridges wrote 150 years ago:

> Love covers, overlooks, speedily forgives and forgets. Full of candor and inventiveness, it puts the best

construction on doubtful matters, searches out any palliation, does not rigidly eye, or wantonly expose (Genesis 9:23), a brother's faults; nor will it uncover them at all, except so far as may be needful for his ultimate good. To refrain from gross slander, while abundant scope is left for needless and unkind detraction, is not covering sin. Nor is the "seven-times forgiveness" the true standard of love, which, like its Divine Author, covers all sins....Oh! let us "put on the Lord Jesus" in his spirit of forbearing, disinterested, sacrificing love—"Even as Christ forgave you, so also do ye."

Chapter Thirteen:
Cultivate Your Fig Tree

"Whoso keepeth the fig tree shall eat the fruit thereof: so he that waiteth on his master shall be honored." --Proverbs 27:18

This verse helps us see the Christian attitude toward human authority. We ought to think of it as one who cultivates a fig tree. The husbandman cultivates the tree in order to eat the fruit of it.

The modern man views authority as a necessary evil that we often have to circumvent in order to accomplish what really needs to be done, or in order to get what we want. This view is thrown at us from every direction, especially in T.V. sitcoms and cop shows.

The Biblical view, set forth in the figure of the fig tree, is that those in authority are a blessing to us, and we will reap the reward, if we cultivate the tree properly. We do this by "praying for them, following their good instruction, and accepting that it is God's will to govern us by their hand." (Heidelberg Catechism, Question 104)

The promise is that if we help them to do their job well, we will be able to do our job well, and will accomplish the things that God has called us to do.

The word "waiteth" means to honor, to worship, as God. It comes from a word meaning "to keep," "to watch," "to preserve," or "to keep safe," and is used with respect to keeping a covenant. This is in line with Hebrews 13:17 and Romans 13:1-4. All authority is from God, and his authority is always to be respected and honored, no matter who wields it.

This doctrine is clear, and is generally accepted by those in the Christian school movement. Just as generally, we often find it difficult to apply in specific situations.

The Bible is inspired in all its parts. Not only is God's plan of salvation revealed in Jesus Christ, but God's structure for our life in his earth is set forth. The latter we may call a Christian philosophy of life, and this philosophy is the Word of God as much as the other.

The life for the Christian is that of a free man in Jesus Christ who freely and gladly submits to the order that God has established. We seek, therefore, to establish homes, churches, and states in terms of God's ultimate authority (Romans 13:1-6). This is necessary, for man at his best on this earth is a sinful being who needs structure in order to function at his most productive. As James Madison put it in the Federalist Papers, "If men were angels, no government would be necessary."

Of course, no authority is perfect, for those in authority are sinful beings. Thus, in the thinking that grew out of the Protestant Reformation, there came a recognition that the power of state government and church government should be divided among many hands in order to protect people from tyranny.

The Biblical principles remain, however, although we call our leaders by different names. Every school has some kind of enabling authority: a school board, a church board, a proprietor, as well as principals or superintendent. There will be several layers of decision makers. In order for the school to be successful, this structure must work efficiently and peacefully.

The authority structure of a school is of a piece. If part of it starts to unravel, soon the whole fabric will be full of holes. Students in the class have three separate authorities that they must deal with almost every day: that of parent, teacher, and principal. Wonderful things will happen in the lives of the children if these three authorities act in harmony with each other and the word of God. A teacher is undermining his own authority in the classroom if he allows himself to undermine the authority of the parents or of his principal.

If a school is characterized by teachers

complaining against the principal, against the school board, or against the parents, the classes will be characterized by students complaining against their teachers. This happens with such regularity that it is almost a certainty: a discontented class is the result of a discontented teacher. Rebellious, griping, backbiting teachers are especially destructive in junior high where so many students are going through a rebellious period of their lives.

Ultimately, all authority depends upon moral authority, the assurance that the leader is right. No government that loses the respect of the people can long endure. Even communist governments were able to remain in power because they were able to convince the majority of the people that they represented a more just and stable order.

Governments can crumble very quickly when they lose that moral edge. Even dictators recognize this and spread a web of lies to appear to be different from what they are.

The implications for school administration is clear, but is not the subject of this chapter. It is clear that griping and slander against those in authority is deadly for the whole institution, for it undermines the moral authority which makes success possible. In undermining his principal's authority, the teacher is undermining his own moral authority.

Satan is much smarter than we are, and if he can persuade us that we will make ourselves look good by griping about our superiors, he will accomplish the ruin of us both.

There are always right and proper ways to handle legitimate grievances, and every institution has procedures for doing this. It does not need to be said that complaints ought to be handled in a loving and Christian manner, but another good rule to follow is this: if it is not worth making a fuss about in the proper way, then it is not worth talking about at all.

The Bible knows nothing about us sitting around, griping and complaining. It knows plenty about us working in faith and obedience, submitting ourselves to one another in the fear of God.

In the Bible, one of the greatest examples of a godly regard for authority is David, who became king over all Israel. He knew that authority was of a piece. Therefore, he refused to lift up his hand against King Saul.

Even though Saul became David's terrible enemy and tried everything he could to have David killed, David never responded in kind. Several times he had an opportunity to kill Saul, but refused to do it. He had faith that God would promote him in due time.

When David became king, there was nothing to sully his own moral authority. He did not have the blood of Saul on his hands, and Saul's relatives and supporters had nothing with which to reproach him.

It was only when David misused his authority in the matter of Uriah that David undermined his own moral authority and began to have trouble in his kingdom, and in his family.

The most common excuse for not using the procedures for handling complaints through proper channels is this: "It wouldn't do any good. Mr. _____ (insert name of principal, pastor, husband, or whoever) will never tolerate any dissent. He just runs things like a dictator." The excuse for slander is simply more slander.

The lesson of all this: If you cultivate your fig tree, you will eat the fruit of it. If you support legitimate authority, good things will happen to you. Help make his job easier. Support and pray for him, and for all in authority. This is, after all, obedience to Scripture as well as good sense, as always (1 Timothy 2:1-4). You must cultivate the fig tree in order to enjoy its fruit.

Chapter Fourteen:
Foreseeing the Evil

"A prudent man foreseeth the evil, and hideth himself: but the simple pass on, and are punished." --Proverbs 22:3

"A prudent man foreseeth the evil, and hideth himself; but the simple pass on, and are punished." --Proverbs 27:12

"Drink waters out of thine own cistern, and running waters out of thine own well." --Proverbs 5:15

"Flee also youthful lusts: but follow righteousness, faith, charity, peace, with them that call on the Lord out of a pure heart." --2 Timothy 2:22

Some have said that anything that God says twice must be important. I would suspect that anything that God says is important, but He says it more than once because of our spiritual stupidity.

During the thirty-some years that I taught kindergarten-college classes it was my sad duty to witness and sometime participate in the discipline of teachers who overstepped the boundaries sexually with their students.

I also observed that there was an increasing sophistication in the knowledge and sexual awareness that students have, which I attribute to the ready availability of movies and publishing and music that glorifies sexuality. I am sure that this has not decreased in the years since I have been teaching seminary. The wise teacher will look out for the pitfalls.

In the first place, children are not innocent little saints sexually. "Even a child is known by his doings, whether his work be pure, and whether it be right" (Proverbs 20:11). Some little girls just entering puberty are quite sophisticated and may be already experimenting with siblings, cousins, etc. Likewise the young boys although the experimenting may come later. There are fewer barriers today than in years past.

Junior high and high school "crushes" have always been a trap for teachers, but I expect they are worse today. In your teacher training you were given ways to avoid these crushes and you should look over that material again. Of course a good teacher has affection for his/her students but it is easy for students (and parents) to misunderstand that affection.

I always followed a "hands off" policy for students. I also would never be alone with a student, male or female, except during school hours, when I would always leave the classroom doors open if I had a conference with a student. I have followed the same policy with female parishioners, and my wife always is with me if I counsel them. Innocence is no defense against evil tongues, and the wise counsellor will be discreet in such matters

But the teacher must be an adult, no matter what the enticement. To overstep the bounds in word or deed is a betrayal of trust, a violation of parental authority, and against the laws of the state and punished by the civil authority.

It is a good school policy, and should be announced that any infraction that is reported will be passed on to the civil authorities, for it is a crime for a person in a position of trust to sexually abuse or harass one in his charge. The state has ways of ferreting out the truth in such matters that the school does not have. It is wise for the teacher to know this and avoid any situation that might be misconstrued. A good reputation in the past will not save the teacher from false accusations, so he must be very careful.

Solomon wrote that his proverbs would "...give subtlety to the simple, to the young man knowledge and discretion" (Proverbs 1:4).

"Subtlety" has both a good sense and a bad sense. It means "guile" in the bad sense and "prudence" in the good sense. It means to keep your head on your shoulders and not play the fool as Jesus said, "Be as wise as serpents and harmless as doves." "Discretion" means "devices" either good or bad. The teacher must be smart enough not to get entangled.

Finally, the apostle warns us "Let not then your good be evil spoken of: For the kingdom of God is not meat and drink; but righteousness, and peace, and joy in the Holy Ghost" (Romans 14:16, 17). If this is true with regard to meats and drink, it is even more vital in such things as your behavior toward the children in your trust.

There is an old story about an old lady who was looking for a chauffeur to drive her to and from town. She lived at the top of a hill with a long, narrow, winding driveway. She asked the first applicant how close he could drive near the edge without falling off.

"Oh," he replied. "I am very good and could drive two feet from the edge all the way down."

The second applicant replied to the same question, "Ma'am, I could drive within one foot of the edge and there would be no danger; you would be completely safe."

The third one replied. "Ma'am. I would stay as far away from that cliff as I could." He was hired by the wise old lady.

Good advice for school teachers trying to navigate the thorny wilderness of education.

Chapter Fifteen:
The Unification of Knowledge

"Then shall they call upon me, but I will not answer; they shall seek me early, but they shall not find me: For that they hated knowledge, and did not choose the fear of the LORD: They would none of my counsel: they despised all my reproof" --Proverbs 1:28-30

"Then shalt thou understand the fear of the LORD, and find the knowledge of God." -- Proverbs 2:5

"The fear of the LORD is to hate evil: pride, and arrogancy, and the evil way, and the froward mouth, do I hate." -- Proverbs 8:13

"The fear of the LORD is the beginning of wisdom: and the knowledge of the holy is understanding." -- Proverbs 9:10

"The fear of the LORD prolongeth days: but the years of the wicked shall be shortened." -- Proverbs 10:27

Fountain of Life "The fear of the LORD is a fountain of life to depart from the snares of death" (Proverbs 14:27). The phrase "the fear of the Lord" appears no less than fifteen times in the book of Proverbs and might be called the theme of the book, which sets forth the fruit of this fear.

In fact, the "fear of the Lord" is a phrase that appears throughout the Bible and becomes descriptive of the church: Ac 9:31 "Then had the churches rest throughout all Judaea and Galilee and Samaria, and were edified; and walking in the fear of the Lord, and in the comfort of the Holy Ghost, were multiplied." There are two parts to edification: the "fear of the Lord" and "the comfort of the Holy Ghost."

The first, the fear of the Lord, has to do with God and the relationship of the soul with Him. It includes reverence, repentance, and faith. These things must be part and parcel of the life of the school teacher, and all things must be related to God and His creation, for God is to be all in all. It is this fear, taught by the Holy Scriptures that unifies the curriculum and rejoices the hearts of the children of God no matter how young.

This fear cannot be taught by the precept of men (Isaiah 29:23). This reverence, this repentance, this faith comes only by the Holy Scriptures taught by those fear God (2 Timothy 3:16; Romans 10:17). Hence, teachers must be good workmen in the Scriptures for this truth should underlie all they do. In the Christian School a strong Bible program is essential if the children are to learn the fear of the

Lord. This does not mean preaching all the time, but having the truth penetrate everything.

Paul put it this way: "...receive with meekness the engrafted word, which is able to save your souls" (James 1:21b). The Scriptures must become as natural to you as your daily bread, yea even more than your necessary food. Job, who perhaps did not have blessings of the written Scriptures put it this way, "Neither have I gone back from the commandment of his lips; I have esteemed the words of his mouth more than my necessary food" (Job 23:1).

The second part of edification is "the comfort of the Holy Spirit." This is neatly summarized in the Heidelberg Catechism, Question 1.

Question 1: What is your only comfort in life and in death?

Answer 1: "That I, with body and soul, both in life and in death, am not my own, but belong to my faithful Savior Jesus Christ, who with His precious blood has fully satisfied for all my sins, and redeemed me from all the power of the devil; and so preserves me that without the will of my Father in heaven not a hair can fall from my head; indeed, that all things must work together for my salvation.

Wherefore, by His Holy Spirit, He also assures me of eternal life, and makes me heartily willing and ready from now on to live unto Him."

This blessed assurance will go with a child all of his life, in spite of the vicissitudes of life. He may wander, but he will know where home is, and how to get back to His heavenly Father. This can only come by the work of the Holy Spirit through the Scriptures.

No wonder that "In the fear of the LORD is strong confidence: and his children shall have a place of refuge" (Proverbs 14:26).

The fear of the Lord is not only the "beginning" of wisdom, it is also the "instruction" of wisdom, for before honor is humility. "Wherefore he saith, God resisteth the proud, but giveth grace unto the humble" (James 4:6b).

The right knowledge and the fear of God go together and cannot be separated. The ignorant person cannot truly fear the Lord. Jesus said to the woman of Samaria, "Ye know not what ye worship." The Jew had both the advantage and the greater responsibility: "We know what we worship, for salvation is of the Jew" (John 4).

Solomon knew the connection between the fear of God and the knowledge of God when he wrote,

"They hated knowledge, and did not choose the fear of the LORD..." (Proverbs 1:19). And, "Then thou shall understand the fear of the LORD and find the knowledge of God" (Proverbs 2:5).

The fear of the Lord has a value system: "The fear of the LORD is to hate evil: pride, and arrogancy, and the evil way, and the froward mouth, do I hate Proverbs 8:13)." "By mercy and truth iniquity is purged: and by the fear of the LORD men depart from evil" (Proverbs 16:16). Children must be taught right from wrong, and this is modeled by the teacher more than from the curriculum. If the teacher is aware there will be many opportunities to teach courtesy, compassion, honest, kindness, respect for authority, etc., demonstrating that Christians are a holy people, who have been called out of darkness into his marvelous light (1 Peter 2:9).

The fear of the Lord and the "Knowledge of the holy" are closely related: "The fear of the LORD is the beginning of wisdom: and the knowledge of the holy is understanding" (Proverbs 9:10).

God is like no other. As the Creator He brought forth the universe from nothing, speaking all things into existence. The Second Person of the Trinity is the eternal Word, the Wisdom of God by whom and through whom all things consist. Because of this, the universe is not a collection of random events, nor is man's life without purpose or design. This is put forth in many places of the Scripture, but especially in Psalm 19.

Every teacher would do well to study Psalm 19 in connection with epistemology, or the science of knowledge. The three legs of the communication of knowledge are Creation (vs. 1-7); the Scripture (vs. 8-11); the Holy Spirit who by the Gospel convicts me of error with regard to the message of both Creation and Scripture (vs 12-14). Creation, Scripture, and the Holy Spirit speak with one voice, the Voice of the Almighty God and the school must be in tune with the truth that is revealed by each. In fact Psalm 19 follows the main divisions of the Apostles Creed: The Father and Creation; the Son and Scripture; the Holy Spirit and personal illumination of both Creation and Scripture.

Language itself reflects this unity. A child bumps his head on a rock, and learns the word "rock," for a hard enduring substance. Later on, very early, he will learn to abstract the word rock, so that he can understand when he hears that his daddy's muscles are like a rock. The Bible is full of such abstractions, or figures of speech. Jesus is a shepherd, a door, a lamb, a hen, etc. God is a Father, a King, a judge, an Eagle, a Fortress, a Mountain, etc.

This means God, using words of visible reality expresses truth concerning invisible reality, which in turn means that Scripture speaks words of truth, using both the concrete and the figurative to tell the truth about spiritual things.

But because of sin, the heart is blinded. This blindness does not blind me to abstraction, for I can still understand when somebody says, "She swims like a fish," that it doesn't mean she has fins and gills. But sin does blind me to the truth that God is invisible and I lapse into idolatry, thinking that because the stars give off light they are to be worshipped as gods or God is to be worshipped in them. It takes the Holy Spirit to cleanse me from idolatry.

This is the reason that the Psalmist could pray, "Let the words of my mouth, and the meditation of my heart, be acceptable in thy sight, O Lord, my strength, and my redeemer" (Psalm 19:14). There is much more here that the thoughtful teacher will discover and use to enrich her teaching.

What a wonderful description the prophet gives of the Lord Jesus, and how we find it exemplified in His life and work:

"And the spirit of the LORD shall rest upon him, the spirit of wisdom and understanding, the spirit of counsel and might, the spirit of knowledge and of the fear of the LORD; And shall make him of quick understanding in the fear of the LORD: and he shall not judge after the sight of his eyes, neither reprove after the hearing of his ears: And wisdom and knowledge shall be the stability of thy times, and strength of salvation: the fear of the LORD is his treasure" (Isaiah 33:2, 3, 6).

Appendix: Aphorisms and Notes

There is a form of godliness that denies power to God and invests it in man, that man must release the power of God before God can act. This is humanism with sugar coating.

******

When I hear people complain about strict theology, I know they have just had a discussion with a Reformed Christian and lost. Did you ever hear anyone complain that a doctor had strict medical knowledge, or an engineer knew too much about math. Of course, going to heaven is a lot easier than building a bridge or curing a rash, isn't it? Any sincere person can do it.

******

I do not think that self-expression can be destroyed. Everything that anybody does anywhere shouts, "Sir, I exist," even if the universe responds cynically and futilely [because of the curse of sin), "That, however, does not create in me a sense of responsibility." The self does not depend upon the universe, but upon God, and THAT cannot be undone. Self and property, being alike the creatures of God are indelibly connected by the Eighth Commandment. "Mine, by right from God, not yours" each man says of his wife, his children, his time, his wage, his god, and his contentment. Cannot be undone.

******

Some thoughts for my brothers and sisters in the teaching ministry of the church, if so be it that they would be edified by any of my thoughts.

1. I believe that creation is a perfect if not a complete revelation of the attributes of God. Even before the fall, natural revelation did not stand alone; the meaning of the Tree in the midst of the Garden was not to be found in the tree itself, but in God's word concerning the tree. Hence, man could consume the fruit of any of the trees, but not that one in the midst of the Garden.

But man, then, like man now, had to have it all. God's word defined the covenantal relationship that was to exist between creation and man. Everything is God's and is to be used according to His commandment. Study of Scripture must go hand in hand with the study of the universe, or we are the blind leading the blind.

2. I believe that facts do not speak for themselves, but without scripture may often appear to be something very different from what they are. To Nabal, David was simply a servant that had run away from his master. To the Jews, Jesus was just a pretender who promised salvation but could not save himself. You will find many examples in Scripture.

3. I believe that we must take care of the body if the mind and soul are to be healthy. It does no good to tell the poor to depart and be warmed and fed if you do not give him something to eat. But just as what goes in cannot defile the man, neither can it purify the man. The soul can be purified only by the seed of the Word of God and newness of life (1 Peter 1ff)

4. The poor are not blessed because they are poor. Luke 6:20 must be read in connection with Matthew 5:3, for Jesus is addressing the same people. Those poor in economics are not necessarily poor in spirit and the rich are not necessarily rich in spirit. Those rich in spirit pretend that they must earn their own salvation, and a great many poor folk are very arrogant in this; Those poor in spirit do not bring anything to the table as far as their salvation is concerned and

their father in faith, Abraham, was a very wealthy man. What does God care about silver and gold? the cattle on a thousand hills are His.

******

Ecclesiastes 10:2 "A wise man's heart is at his right hand; but a fool's heart at his left."

In other words, a wise man knows how to employ his heart so as to be profitable and loving. The fool doesn't, but is awkward and brutal. As the left handed person seems awkward to the righty, so the wise man sees how foolish the fool is. Even the tender mercies of the wicked are cruel (Proverbs 12:10).

You have to have your heart in the right place; given over and kept by Christ.

******

God is so good, that no human is without a witness for the whole law and prophets are written on the heart of every man. Jesus said. How are you to treat your fellow? with the same passion and definition that you desire to be treated Jesus said that was the sum of the law and the prophets "Therefore all things whatsoever ye would that men should do to you, do ye even so to them: for this is the law and the prophets (Matthew 7:12)."

How different the world would be if we understood this. Paul unpacked this in Philippians 2:1-11, giving the example of the Lord Jesus.

This proves the existence of the soul, distinct from the body, and in the image of God. It also proves our bondage to sin, for every man seeks his own way and his own things, this writer included, but I am not what I was when I was 17 years old, thank God.

******

How do you defend the reasonableness of agnosticism? Isn't agnosticism a claim to know what everybody knows? How you deny knowledge to everybody without knowing everything that everybody knows? And then you strut as though you did? Atheism is simply a PhD in Agnosticism at the school of Fools and Charlatans. Jesus said, "And every one that heareth these sayings of mine, and doeth them not, shall be likened unto a foolish man, which built his house upon the sand" (Matthew 7:26): Jesus affirmed that foolishness is something to be avoided, and there is nothing more foolish than being wise in your own conceits, [opinions], and thinking you are doing something important while you build upon sand and human arrogance.

******

He had carefully prepared for the moment. The steaks and salads were wonderful. Dessert was being served when the music and flowers were delivered. The moment had come.

He took her hand in his and gazed into her eyes. "Will you marry me?" he said softly. She replied, "but there is something you haven't told me. Do you love me?"

"Of course," he replied. "I love everybody."

FAIL

Isaiah 61:10: "I will greatly rejoice in the LORD, my soul shall be joyful in my God; for he hath clothed me with the garments of salvation, he hath covered me with the robe of righteousness, as a bridegroom decketh himself with ornaments, and as a bride adorneth herself with her jewels."

Index

Easier to become a
Christian, *41*
Ecclesiastes 1:15 and
7:13, 51
Ecclesiastes 10:2, 108
Ecclesiastes 12:11, g
Ecclesiastes 2, 14
Ecclesiastes 2:1-8, 14
Ecclesiastes 7:14, 52
Ecclesiastes 7:16,17, 53
Eighth Commandment,
106
Eliab, 64
enabling authority, 88
Enjoyment., 23
environment, 58
Ephesians 4:31,32, 82
Ephesians 4:8-16, 69
Ephesians 6:4, 42
Ephesians 6:9, *10*
equalizing all sins, 50
Esau, *40*
Excited teachers, 34
Exodus 21:23,24, *9*
experience, h
Eye for eye, *9*
Ezekiel 11:19,20, 38
Ezekiel 36:26, 2

facts do not speak for
themselves, 107
family's most precious
possession, 62
fast the time flew, 14
fear of God, 90, 100,
101
fear of the Lord, 97, 98,
99, 100, 101
Federalist Papers, 88
fig tree, 18, 86, 91
Fig Tree, 86
figures of speech, 103
flutter in the mind, 51
form of godliness, 105
fruit, good or evil, 37
Galatians 3:24, 45
Galatians 3:3, 43
Galatians 4:28,29, 44
Galatians 4:4, 19
Galatians 5:16-26, 37
Galatians 5:19-21, 44
Galatians 5:20, 43
Galatians 6:1, 62, 74
Galatians 6:7,8, 44
Gambler, 19
Gen. 9:23, 85
generosity, compassion
and mercy, *11*

51265086R00075

Made in the USA
San Bernardino, CA
17 July 2017